If you know nothing about Astrology, this a difficult read. You must understand Astrology as a whole BEFORE you understand your NATAL CHART. Purchase the textbook ASTROLOGY EXPLAINED to get a deeper grasp on ASTROLOGY. I also offer a course that helps you know Astrology deeper as well. Below are 2 QR CODES. One will be for 50% off Astrology Explained, and the other will be for my online Astrology Course. If you have any questions, please email me: hoodmystic@gmail.com.

Scan your Phone Camera over these images to access the links provided and enjoy.

Astrology Courses

Astrology Explained

How to Read Natal Charts Easily and Effectively
By Kyree Anthony

The Purpose of this Workbook	**2**
The Planets & Constellations & Houses & Keywords	**5**
How To Use This Workbook	**9**
Worksheets	**14**
Example Worksheet	**21**
Appendix & Glossary	**24**

The Purpose of this Workbook

The Study of Stars through astrology allows you to study your divinity and sovereignty.

To Study the Stars, you need calculation and observation. This workbook will help you calculate your birth chart and translate those calculations. Understanding the link between the macro and microcosmic relationship between us and the stars can develop a deeper purpose for ourselves. The purpose of this workbook is to bring out your creative, conscious, magical, noble, sublime, free, independent, shining, glorious self. Astrology also helps us reveal the hidden motives and allows us to bring more control into our lives.

What can be learned from Astrology is the ability to release psychological tension. Psychological tension is our humanity vs. our divinity. In Astrology, we remember our divine aspects and learn how to apply them to our daily life. In this, we are reducing our psychological tension through the divination practice of astrology.

Consistency is the main ingredient to understanding Astrology. Without feeling and persistence, you will give up without giving yourself a chance. I learned Astrology by not giving up and taking it one day at a time. This workbook is a guide, but it will not be consistent for you. Take notes and when you reach your limit, put the book down. When you are ready to learn again, pick it back up. Remembering the stars' language is easy. Being patient and allowing ourselves time to learn is challenging. Find balance with taking this book in chunks and learning at your own pace.

By understanding the planets and constellations, planets and constellations will know you, and from this relationship or correspondence, you create more control of your life and destiny.

The idea of this workbook is to create a conversation where there was never a conversation within. If there is an ulterior motive outside of understanding yourself in the context of Astrology, then this workbook will not be practical. The most effective way to understand this workbook is to have the intention to learn and make sense of your natal chart. If you create a language that resonates with you to understand your natal chart, your natal chart will become a map you can utilize to navigate the inner world. The planetary movements and internal dialogue are synonymous. They are both unseen and abstract. They only manifest as a reality through our expression and works. For most of us, we simply operate on autopilot mode and merely expect things out of life. This workbook can take you out of autopilot into being the architect for your life if taken seriously.

I created a simple system that, if implemented and understood, can change your life. We are working with the premise that changing your outer world is done by changing your inner world. So let us know that inner world.

Included will be an example of utilizing this workbook using my chart to understand your chart and aspects.

All you need to do is get a copy of your birth chart to enter the information into the worksheets provided, utilize the appendix to formulate meanings for each planet(sign & house), and recreate your chart using senses you can understand. By doing this, you will have a full grasp of your map, and you don't have to pay astrologers hundreds of dollars to get information based on their understanding alone. Likewise, you don't have to understand your chart on internet programs with pre-programmed responses that never factor you personally. We all can appreciate our map, and this workbook helps you get there.

It is essential to understand your chart using your vocabulary. This workbook is a tool to assist you in connecting the dots of your Astrology Chart.

Astrology is the meaningful relationship between your experience and the positions of the celestial bodies. You can systematically determine this relationship.

Astrology is a form of divination[1] by using the stars to understand specific blockages and advantages you can exploit for your higher good.

The only way to understand Astrology is to know how to analyze your chart and understand it. This course will bring you closer to understanding your chart for yourself.

We will use a Geocentric Model and use the Earth(Heart) as the center of your experience and base the positions of celestial bodies related to you. In this workbook, we will focus on the first nine planets in astrology. After that, we will discuss the nodes and the asteroids if a more transparent view is required after completing this workbook in later volumes.

---

[1] "act of foretelling by supernatural or magical means the future, or discovering what is hidden or obscure," https://www.etymonline.com/word/divination

We start with you being the observer or Astrologer, understanding the stars' geometric positions and constellations, and figuring out what they mean to create our language surrounding what is observed.

The Planets & Constellations & Houses & Keywords

The Planets in our Solar System play an important role in understanding Astrology. We can understand the subtle but significant changes externally and internally by tracking the movement across the sky and relating them to human experience. The Planets' movements are varied. While some move daily, others take weeks to make any changes.

Five planets are visible to the naked eye: Mercury, Venus, Mars, Jupiter, and Saturn. Astronomers discovered Uranus, Neptune, and Pluto. Together with Earth, they make up the nine planets of our solar system. It is interesting to note that when astrologers use the term "planets," they include the Sun and Moon.[2]

Also, be sure to check the appendix for more help with formulating keywords.

Planet - Meaning - (time in each constellation)
Moon - intuition - and perception (2 - 3 days)
Sun - Bringer of energy - What you are willing to give (Month)
Mercury - the messenger of truth - refinement (3 - 4 weeks)
Venus - Response, attention, cherishing, and potential (4 - 5 weeks)
Mars - Active, Action, Athletic Pursuits, Aggression (23 Days to 2 months)
Jupiter - Life Path - The Key, Guide, teacher, guru - Wisdom and growth (12 - 13 months)
Saturn - Law - Prince of the Material World - Structure and Boundaries (2 to 3 years)
Uranus - New manifestation of your energy (5-7 Years)
Neptune -- Is your spiritual Life (10 - 12 years)
Pluto -- Is your spiritual transformation (12 - 15 years)

KEYWORDS OF THE PLANET

THE SUN
BASIC--Individuality, what one is, vitality, will, chief ambitions, those in authority, men.
POSITIVE--Generosity, dignity.
NEGATIVE--Despotism, arrogance, ostentation, lack of ambition, animalistic qualities.

---

[2] http://www.math.nus.edu.sg/aslaksen/projects/kh-urops.pdf

THE MOON
BASIC--Personality, imagination, instinctual mind, emotions, change, fecundation, the people, women.
POSITIVE--Positive psychic qualities, personal magnetism.
NEGATIVE--Negativeness, visionariness, dreaming, vacillation, frivolity, fretfulness, procrastination, indecision, incorrect impressions.

MERCURY
BASIC--Reason; self-expression of all kinds; speaking, writing, gestures; knowledge through reason.
POSITIVE--Quick-wittedness, eloquence, literary ability, talent.
NEGATIVE--Restlessness, gossip, profanity, demagogy, dishonesty, deceit, nervousness, worry, indecision, forgetfulness, clumsiness.

VENUS
BASIC--Attraction, cohesion, coalition, personal love, social instincts and activities, art, ornamentation, beauty.
POSITIVE--Harmony, artistic ability, cheerfulness, suavity.
NEGATIVE--Sensuality, dissoluteness, vulgarity, sloth, laziness, sentimentality, vanity, inconstancy.

MARS
BASIC--Dynamic energy.
POSITIVE--Constructiveness, courage, enterprise, enthusiasm, gallantry.
NEGATIVE--Combativeness, friction, temper, destructiveness, passion, lustfulness, impulsiveness, audacity, coarseness, egotism.

JUPITER
BASIC--Expansion, vision, optimism, creativity, orthodox religious tendencies.
POSITIVE--Benevolence, broad-mindedness, executive ability, legal ability, respect for law, honor, charity, reverence, conservatism, luxury, popularity, success.
NEGATIVE--Overconfidence, extravagance, laziness, wastefulness, showiness, bombast, dissipation, sportiness, lawlessness, procrastination.

SATURN
BASIC--Contraction, persistence, caution.
POSITIVE--Faithfulness, stability, concentration, analysis system, building qualities, tact, diplomacy, justice, thrift, economy, deliberation, conservatism, endurance, discipline.
NEGATIVE--Crystallization, obstruction, selfishness, slowness, fearfulness, limitation, materialism, melancholy, pessimism, avarice, secretiveness, suspicion, severity, cynicism.

URANUS

BASIC--The Awakener; altruism, inventiveness, originality, sudden action, unconventionality.

POSITIVE--Progressiveness, universality, universal love of humanity, impersonality, independence, love of liberty, romance, intuition.

NEGATIVE--Eccentricity, spasmodic action, bohemianism, fanaticism, irresponsibility, licentiousness, anarchy.

NEPTUNE

BASIC--Superphysical entities of all degrees and impressions from them. Divinity, occultism, knowledge from sources above reason, viz., superphysical beings.

POSITIVE--Spirituality, intuition, inspiration, divination, prophecy, devotion, music.

NEGATIVE--Delusions, chaotic mental conditions, morbidity, fraud, incoherence, deception, dishonesty, mediumship.

PLUTO

BASIC--Renewing, enlivening, breaking open, germinating, erupting, reorganizing, provoking, transition.

POSITIVE--Regeneration, transmutation, positive clairvoyance, revivification, universal welfare, motivation to strive for spiritual power.

NEGATIVE--Force, defiance, death, destruction, fanaticism, struggle, sensuality, regimentation, underworld, black magic, decomposition.

The Constellations - Meaning

Aries - Masculine | Creativity
Taurus - Feminine | Beauty
Gemini - Spiritual | Communication
Cancer - Feminine | Family and Wealth
Leo - Masculine | Creativity
Virgo - Feminine | Intelligence
Libra - Spiritual | Relationship and Commitment
Scorpio - Feminine | Sex and Money
Sagittarius - Spiritual | Travel and Education
Capricorn - Masculine | Career and Goal Setting
Aquarius - Spiritual | Community
Pisces - Masculine | Feminine | Rulership

Houses[3]

1st.--Beginnings, early environment, personality, physical body
2nd.-- Finance, the freedom given by money

---

[3] https://www.rosicrucian.com/aks/akseng01.htm

3rd.-- Lower mind and speaking, short journeys, brothers and sisters

4th.-- The home, the mother, conditions at the end of life, lands, and mines

5th.-- Pleasure, education, children, publications, speculation

6th.-- Service, relations with employers and employees, health and sickness

7th.-- Partnership, marriage, the public

8th.-- Legacies, cause of death, occult tragedy, regeneration

9th.-- Higher mind, religion, law, long journeys

10th.-- Profession, standing in the community, the father

11th.-- Friends, hopes, and wishes

12th.-- Paying debts of destiny, limitations, institutions for the care of unfortunates, secrecy, mysticism

How To Use This Workbook

Translating your chart is based on the understanding that we need to bring astrology from abstract to something we can understand. Keywords help us simplify this process and create a language we can build upon for our future study.

It's important to understand that each planetary aspect has light and darkness associated with it. Light is made aware, and dark is unaware. So when crafting your translation, factor in the positives and negatives to create a unique understanding. By adding up each meaning, we develop a sense of each planet based on our perspective. Then, use the resources provided in the appendix to create a concrete understanding of the keywords you want to use.

The goal is to learn astrology using your language and not astrologese[4]. This Workbook will allow you to understand your chart intimately. Once completed, focus on what you need to work on, highlight goals, and test this formula out. If you have any questions about this workbook, feel free to email me at **hoodmystic@gmail.com.**

M = Meaning
The formula is as follows: (M + M + M = What this planet means in your chart in your words) Reference the appendix to create keywords for each Planet, Sign, and House in the first chart. Form those keywords to create a complete sentence in the following chart. Then, in *repeating signs and houses, find different synonyms to develop an additional dialogue related to that specific planet.*

---

[4] The jargon used by astrologers.

Planet	Meaning	Sign	Meaning	House	Meaning
Moon	I Feel				
Sun	I am				
Mercury	I think				
Venus	I love				
Mars	I act				
Jupiter	I expand				
Saturn	I constrict				
Neptune	I am inspired				
Uranus	I am awakened				
Pluto	I am transformed				
Rising	I am seen as				

Creating synonyms is not an easy thing to do at first. First, you have to learn to use the words as prompts. Then, when referencing how you feel, state how you think, and allow yourself to edit as necessary.

Planet	What this planet means in your chart in your words
Moon	
Sun	
Mercury	
Venus	
Mars	
Jupiter	
Saturn	

Neptune	
Uranus	
Pluto	
Rising	

Once you map out your chart on the above tables and create a translation for your Chart, you are ready to understand your aspects. Aspects are the Actions associated with the Planets in your Chart. Using a simple formula, you can appreciate the things you need to work on and what you are exceptional in but may not be aware of.

Aspect	Action
Trine	Natural and Easy Energy
Sextile	Assistance, Cooperation
Square	Obstruction, Inharmony
Opposition	Issues that you Can Resolve
Conjunction	Harmonious or Conflicting

Now reference your chart, identify the aspects, and record them in the table above, not as astrological signs, but enter your translations for each planetary placement. (In the Worksheet section, there will be a more extended version of this Table if needed.) Feel free to create a larger table on the poster board. You can use these tables as the framework to utilize the formula being presented. Once you record the translations and aspects, take some time to create an equation. The aspect chart helps you see what areas are favorable, what things you have issues with and need to work on, what you need to let go of, and your strengths and weaknesses. The goal of the aspect table is to create a realistic view of yourself. Utilizing the Therefore, always resolving effective positive and negative aspects will give you a clearer picture of yourself. *Also included is an example of how to understand this worksheet using my chart.*

What you will find here are difficulties, strengths, and weaknesses. The more honest you are in this process, the more revealing this section will be. This section will allow you to see how these planets interplay in your own words.

Reference your chart for the list of aspects. Most online chart generators come with a list of elements. They may not explain them, so this is where this table comes in handy. Be honest and critical in formulating your equations. In processing your equations, you will find issues. The goal is to provide solutions that combat the issues squares, oppositions, and sometimes conjunctions present. **purposes**

Translation of Planet	Aspect	Translation of Planet	Equation

Worksheets

Your Natal Chart Translation

Planet	Meaning	Sign	Meaning	House	Meaning
Moon	Emotional State				
Sun	Expression				
Mercury	Mental				
Venus	Attention				
Mars	Creative Action				
Jupiter	Perspective				

Saturn	Protection				
Neptune	Spiritual Development				
Uranus	Conscious Truth				
Pluto	Power and Wealth				
Rising	How the World Sees the person/place /event				

Write out each meaning in sentence form utilizing the definitions you created for each sign and house.

My Planet Meanings

Planet	What this planet means in your chart in your words
Moon	
Sun	
Mercury	
Venus	
Mars	
Jupiter	
Saturn	
Neptune	

Uranus	
Pluto	
Rising	

My Natal Chart Translation

After filling out the table to your best ability, write a paragraph using the meanings provided to get a better view of yourself.

How to Read Natal Charts Easily and Effectively

My Aspects

After coming up with your equations for each aspect in your chart. Write a paragraph utilizing each equation to get a holistic view on your strengths and weaknesses. The effort you put into this document will equate to what you get out of this.

Example Worksheet

I will reference my chart. I am using a sidereal chart. Feel free to use whatever map makes you feel comfortable. I visited Astro-Seek.com to get a copy of my chart.

My Planets

Planet	Meaning	Sign	Meaning	House	Meaning
Moon	I Feel	Gemini	Other People	9th	Spiritual Life
Sun	I am	Leo	Leader	11th	Group
Mercury	I think	Leo	Authority	11th	Collective
Venus	I love	Leo	Importance	11th	Friends
Mars	I act	Scorpio	Sex	2nd	Possession
Jupiter	I expand	Sagittarius	pathworking	3rd	Communication
Saturn	I constrict	Libra	fairness	1st	The ego
Neptune	I am inspired	Sagittarius	science	3rd	communication
Uranus	I am awakened	Scorpio	transformation	2nd	Daily routine
Pluto	I am transformed	Libra	Artistic	1st	Self
Rising	I am seen as	Virgo	Perfectionist	1st	Self

Write out each meaning in sentence form utilizing the purposes you created for each sign and house. This is not an easy thing to do. First, you have to learn to use the words as prompts. When referencing how you feel, state how you think, and allow yourself to edit as necessary.

My Planet Meanings

Planet	What this planet means in your chart in your words
Moon	I feel spiritually centered when I am exploring duality.
Sun	I am the leader of my group or social circle.
Mercury	I think as an authority for the collective.
Venus	I love being essential to my friends.
Mars	My sexual energy is a valued possession.
Jupiter	My path expands through communication.
Saturn	My ego's sense of fairness limits me.
Neptune	The science of communication inspires me.
Uranus	The daily routine of transformation will lead to my overall awakening.
Pluto	I bring to light my artistic self.
Rising	People may see me as a perfectionist.

My Aspects Translated

Aspect	Action
Trine	Natural and Easy Energy
Sextile	Assistance, Cooperation
Square	Obstruction, Inharmony
Opposition	Issues that Can be Resolved

Conjunction	Harmonious or Conflicting

Aspect	Translation of Planet	Aspect Action	Translation of Planet
Neptune Sextile Pluto	The science of communication inspires me.	Assists	I am transformed by bringing to light my artistic self.
Mercury Square Uranus	I think as an authority for the collective.	Inharmony	The daily routine of transformation will lead to my overall awakening.
Mars Conjunct Uranus	My sexual energy is a valued possession.	Conflicting	The daily routine of transformation will lead to my overall awakening.
Sun Trine Neptune	I am the leader of my group or social circle.	Natural and Easy Energy	The science of communication inspires me.
Moon Trine Saturn	I feel spiritually centered when I am exploring duality.	Easy Energy	My ego's sense of fairness limits me.

Aspect	Equation (complete sentence)
Neptune Sextile Pluto	Learning how to communicate will assist in my transformation. Always concentrate on effectively communicating to get to the proper change.
Mercury Square Uranus	Thoughts of authority take me out of my daily routine. Authority comes from following a daily routine.
Mars Conjunct Uranus	My sexual energy disrupts my daily routine. By processing my sexual life, I will have more power to awaken myself to my transformation.
Sun Trine Neptune	Scientific communication will lead me to be an authority amongst my social group. Therefore, effectivel Can resolve effective communication will empower me.

Appendix & Glossary

Astrology	"calculation and foretelling based on observation of heavenly bodies,"
Birth/Natal Chart	An astrology birth chart—also called an astrology natal chart—is a map of where all the planets were in their journey around the Sun (from our vantage point on earth) at the exact moment you were born.
Conjunctions	Two or more planets are sitting next to each other. Conjunction gives excellent strength to the energies of the interacting planets.
Constellations	"position of a planet in the zodiac;."
Oppositions	The opposition is when planets are exactly opposite each other in the chart wheel. Oppositions create stress.
Planets	"wandering (stars),"
Sextiles	The sextile planetary aspect represents a certain 60° angle between two planets in the natal chart in astrology. Thus, the energy created between these two planets with a sextile element is a very cooperative one.
Trines	In astrology, the trine planetary aspect occurs when two planets are in synchronicity with one another.

Table of Astrological Characteristics of the Planets

(From "Making Sense Of Astrology")

Sun — Life force, self-esteem, power and ambition, authority (the father); heart, circulation, eyes. — **Force**

Moon — Sensitivity, inspiration, confusion, exaggeration; chaos, psychology. — **Subconscious**

Mercury — Intellect, ability to adapt; nervous system, brain, speech organs. — **Communication**

Venus — Emotions, eroticism, artistic ability, relationships, world of art; organs of smell and touch. — **Harmony**

Mars — Energy, desire, choleric temperament, courage, force, military and technical world; muscular system, blood, genitals. — **Energy**

Jupiter — Philosophical and religious thought, nomadic nature, financial and judicial world; liver, lungs. — **Expansion**

Saturn — Concentration, melancholic temperament, earth, soil, lonely places; bones, skin. — **Concentration**

Uranus — Intuition, independence, engineering, revolution, occultism. — **Crisis**

Neptune — Fertility, metabolism, subconscious, consciousness, emotions (the mother); stomach, belly, uterus. — **Inspiration**

Pluto — Turning points, crisis, death. — **Turning Point**

Sun Lifeforce. Self-esteem. Power and ambition. Authority (the father): heart. Circulation, eyes.
Moon Sensitivity, inspiration, confusion, exaggeration, chaos, psychology.
Mercury Intellect. ability to adapt: nervous system, brain. Speech organs.
Venus Emotions. Eroticism, artistic ability. Relationships. World of art: organs of smell and touch.
Mars Energy. Desire. Choleric temperament. Courage, force. Military and technical world: muscular system. Blood. Genitals.
Jupiter Philosophical and religious thought, nomadic nature. Expansion of the financial and judicial world, fiver. Lungs.
Saturn Concentration. Melancholic temperament, earth, skin, Concentration, lonely places; bones. skin
Uranus Intuition. Independence. Engineering. Revolution. occultism
Neptune Fertility, metabolism, subconscious, consciousness, emotions (the mother): stomach, belly, uterus
Pluto Turning points. Crisis. Death. Crisis Inspiration

The planets and what they symbolize

The Sun - I am

The Moon - I feel

Mercury - I think

Venus - I love

Mars - I act

Jupiter - I expand

Saturn - I constrict (boundaries)

Uranus - I awaken

Neptune - I am not the illusion

Pluto - I am the soul/spirit

The Sun - I am   Jupiter - I expand
The Moon - I feel   Saturn I constrict (boundaries)
Mercury - I Think   Uranus I - Awaken
Venus - I love   Neptune - I am not the illusion
Mars - I act   Pluto - I am the soul/spirit

Latin Name	English Name	Characteristics
Aries	Ram	Energy, activity, entrepreneurship.
Taurus	Bull	Materialism, practical sense, perseverance.
Gemini	Twins	Communication, social activities.
Cancer	Crab	Social work, caring professions.
Leo	Lion	Authority, leadership, vitality.
Virgo	Virgin	Scientific, analytical ability.
Libra	Scales	Artistic, sense of equilibrium, mediation.
Scorpio	Scorpion	Sex, medicine, science, intensity.
Sagittarius	Archer	Sports, idealism, religion, philosophy.
Capricorn	Goat	Ambition, politics.
Aquarius	Water Bearer	Humane, intuitive.
Pisces	Fishes	Dreamer, altruistic.

Aries Ram Energy. Activity. Entrepreneurship

Taurus Bull Materialism. Practical sense. perseverance

Gemini Twins Communication, social activities

Cancer Crab Social work, caring professions

Leo Lion Authority. Leadership. vitality

Virgo Virgin Scientific. analytical ability

Libra Scales Artistic, sense of equilibrium, mediation

Scorpio Scorpion Sex. medicine, science, intensity

Sagittarius Archer Sports. Idealism. Religion. philosophy

Capricorn Goat Ambition. politic

Aquarius Water Bearer Humane, intuitive

Pisces Fishes Dreamer, altruistic

Constellations and what the symbolize

Aries - initiation

Taurus - manifestation

Gemini - duality

Cancer - family/protection

Leo - individuality

Virgo - perfection

Libra - balance

Scorpio - birth, renewal, transformation

Sagittarius - pathworking

Capricorn - ascension

Aquarius - discovery

Pisces - awareness of your soul

Aries - Initiation   Libra - Balance
Taurus - manifestation Scorpio - birth, renewal, transformation
Gemini - Duality Sagittarius - pathworking
Cancer - Family/Protection Sagittarius - Pathworking
Leo - Individuality Aquarius - Discovery
Virgo - Perfection Pisces - Awareness of your soul

Number of the House	Characteristics
I	Personality, body type, the person, the ego.
II	Financial means, possessions, economics, wages.
III	Next of kin, brothers, sisters, neighbours.
IV	Parents, the home, ancestors, real estate, agriculture.
V	One's own children, education, love life.
VI	Wage labour, military service, health.
VII	Social relations, marriage, politics, partners, enemies.
VIII	Death, burial and things connected with it, legacies, occultism and mysticism.
IX	Spiritual life, religions, philosophy, long travels.
X	Social status, profession, honour, fame.
XI	Friends, social life.
XII	Confinement, illness, seclusion, loneliness, secrets, crime.

Ari

I Personality, body type, person, the ego
II Financial means, possessions, economics, wages
III Next of kin, brothers, sisters, neighbors
IV Parents, the home, ancestors, real estate, agriculture
V (one's children, education, love life
VI Wage labor. military service, health
VII Social relations. Marriage, politics. partners, enemies
VIII Death, burial, and things connected with its legacies. occultism and mysticism
IX Spiritual life. religions, philosophy, long travels
X Social status, profession, honor. fame
XI Friends. social lite
XII Confinement, illness, seclusion, loneliness, secrets. crime

Rising Sign and MC meaning

Your **Rising** Sign. Your **rising** sign—also known as your **ascendant**, represents how others see you, your general impression of people, and your spontaneous reactions. It reflects the Zodiacal sign that was ascending on the eastern horizon the moment you were born.

The Midheaven (MC or Medium Coeli, literally 'middle of the sky') is one of the essential birth chart angles. It traditionally indicates career, status, aim in life, aspirations, public reputation, and life goal.

		ASPECT	ANGLE	SYMBOL	NATURE	PSYCHOLOGICAL MEANING
HARMONIC ASPECTS	TOOLS	TRINE	120°	△	♃	TUNING – COMFORT DEVELOPING – ENERGY FLOWING INNATE ABILITY SLOW CONSTANT ACTION
		SEXTILE	60°	✳	♀	COMPLEMENTARITY ENERGY EXCHANGE CREATION IMMEDIATE PRODUCTIVE REACTION
DYNAMIC ASPECTS	CHALLENGES	OPPOSITION	180°	☍	♄	CONTRAST – EFFORT PRESSION – STRESS PASSIONAL ATTRACTION SLOW CONSTANT ACTION
		SQUARE	90°	□	♂	LACERATION – TENSION ACTION/REACTION EMOTIVE EARTHQUAKE IRRECONCILABILITY
NEUTRAL ASPECTS	?	CONJUNCTION	0°	♂	×	UNION – CONCENTRATION ENERGIES FUSION BINDING ACTION

PSYCHOLOGICAL MEANING
Trine TUNING - COMFORT DEVELOPING - ENERGY FLOWING INNATE ABILITY SLOW CONSTANT ACTION
Sextile COMPLEMENTARITY ENERGY EXCHANGE CREATION IMMEDIATE PRODUCTIVE REACTION
Opposition CONTRAST - EFFORT PRESSION - STRESS PASSIONAL ATTRACTION SLOW CONSTANT ACTION
Square LACERATION - TENSION ACTION/REACTION EMOTIVE EARTHQUAKE IRRECONCILABILITY
Conjunction UNION - CONCENTRATION ENERGIES FUSION BINDING ACTION

Printed in Great Britain
by Amazon